Exploring Earth's Resources

Using Water

Sharon Katz Cooper

Heinemann Library
Chicago, Illinois

Designed by Michelle Lisseter
Printed and bound in China, by South China Printing Company

11 10 09 08 07
10 9 8 7 6 5 4 3 2 1

Library of Congress Cataloging-in-Publication Data

Katz Cooper, Sharon.
  Using water / Sharon Katz Cooper.
      p. cm. -- (Exploring Earth's resources)
  Includes index.
  ISBN-13: 978-1-4034-9314-9 (lib. bdg. hardcover)
  ISBN-10: 1-4034-9314-6 (lib. bdg. hardcover)
  ISBN-13: 978-1-4034-9322-4 (pbk.)
  ISBN-10: 1-4034-9322-7 (pbk.)
 1. Water--Juvenile literature. I. Title.
  GB662.3.K38 2007
  553.7--dc22

                                    2006029708

Acknowledgments
The publishers would like to thank the following for permission to reproduce photographs:
Alamy pp. **11** (Juniors Bildarchly), **19** (Nature Picture Library); Brand X Pictures p. **8** (Morey
Midbradt); Corbis pp. **4** (NASA), **5** (Reuters/Vladimir Pirogov), **9** (Michael Pole), **12**, **13**
(Kevin Fleming), **21** (Royalty Free); Digital Vision p. **7** (Robert Harding/Jim Reed); Getty
Images pp. **6** (Stone/Robin Smith), **14**, **15** (Akira Kaede), **16** (Photonica), **18** (David Sacks);
Harcourt Education Ltd pp. **22** top and bottom (Tudor Photography); Masterfile p. **17** (Gary
Rhijnsburger); Photolibrary p. **10** (Botanica); Rex-Features p. **20**.

Cover photograph reproduced with permission of Jupiter (Banana Stock).

Every effort has been made to contact copyright holders of any material reproduced in
this book. Any omissions will be rectified in subsequent printings if notice is given to the
publishers.

Contents

Some words are shown in bold, **like this**.
You can find them in the glossary on page 23.

Why Is Water Important?

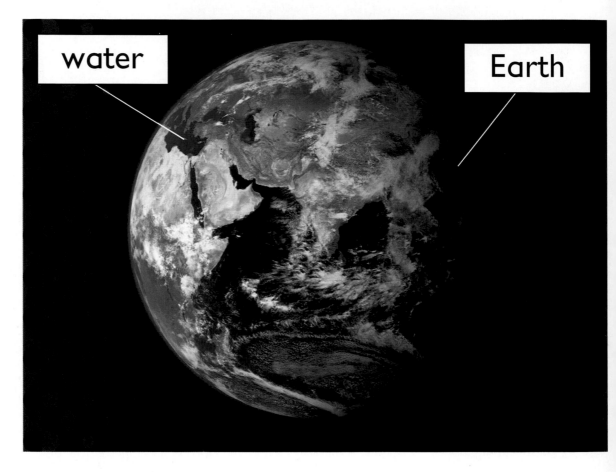

water

Earth

Most of Earth's surface is covered with water.

We use water for almost everything we do.

Water is a **natural resource**.

Natural resources come
from Earth.

Where Does Our Water Come From?

We get water from oceans, rivers, and lakes.

It is found underground, too.

Water is always moving. It travels across the sky as clouds.

It falls to the ground as rain and snow.

Water moves around on Earth's surface.

It flows down hills and mountains.

Water flows through streams and rivers. It flows out into the sea.

The Sun's heat turns it back into clouds.

How Do We Use Water?

Plants, animals, and humans need water to live.

Plants need it to make food.

Animals and humans need to
drink water.

We use water to help us grow
plants for food.

We also get a lot of our food from oceans and from rivers.

We use water to help us move from one place to another.

Many of the things we use each day come to us by ship.

We use water for **energy**.

Dams on large rivers produce electricity. We use electricity to make lights and other machines work.

We use water at home.

We need water for cooking
and cleaning.

We also use water for fun.

We spend time on boats and we go swimming.

Can We Run Out of Water?

Most of Earth's water is in the sea. Seawater is salty.

We cannot use it for drinking or growing plants. We need fresh water.

Some parts of Earth do not have much fresh water.

Without water, people cannot cook, clean, or drink.

Some big cities store water in **reservoirs**.

If a reservoir starts to dry up, we need to try to use less water.

We can turn off water faucets when we are not using them.

We can take quick showers instead of baths. This will use less water.

21

Water Cycle in a Bag!

Want to see how water moves from one place to another? In this activity, you can find out.

1. Fill a plastic cup with water.
2. Place it in a resealable plastic bag.
3. Make sure the bag is closed tightly.
4. Tape the bag to a window in a sunny place. Keep the cup upright.
5. Watch what happens each day. What do you see?

Note: The water **evaporates** from the cup. This means the heat from the Sun turns the water from a liquid into a gas.

Glossary

 **dam** wall that holds back water

 **energy** something that gives power

 **evaporate** to change from a liquid to a gas

 **natural resource** material from Earth that we can use

 **reservoir** large pool for storing water

Index